Gary Jones

Stockholm

Contents

1

Introduction

Sweden is a beautiful country in Europe that is rich in history, art, and culture, and its capital Stockholm is in the heart of its continuing legacy. Over the years, this majestic capital has grown in popularity among tourists. In fact, in 2010 alone, Stockholm welcomed more than ten million overnight stays, which made it the most visited city in all of Scandinavia. People are drawn to the natural beauty of Stockholm, what with it being named Europe's first ever Green Capital by the European Union (EU) Commission. Tourists also come to this city to learn more about the medieval era, of which Stockholm has many stories of. The city's countless museums and art galleries also add to the appeal, and its good food, good beer, and vibrant nightlife put it on top of many people's Must-Visit Cities in Europe list.

If you appreciate nature, love art, and crave delicious food, then Stockholm, Sweden is the right travel destination for you. In just three days, Stockholm will take you on a journey through ages, beginning with its roots in the medieval times and ending with its current position in the contemporary world through its art. Your palette will also enjoy this vacation because Stockholm is the home of comfort food and crazy concoctions. Moreover, if those things are not enough, take pleasure in and unwind with the beautiful view of the city's harbor and well-kept parks.

Through this travel guide, you will find short lists of the best of the best in Stockholm. From affordable accommodations to the most popular restaurants to the museums and galleries you just can't miss, this book has got you covered. Find activities to do and places to visit; be excited by the nightlife and satiate yourself with a cup of fika (coffee). There is even a three-day itinerary included at the end of this book to give you an idea of how much you can do while visiting this beautiful and historical European city.

Note, also that all prices listed on this book are rounded to the nearest dollar value. I hope that this will make budgeting for your travel a lot easier.

And so, without further ado, here is your travel guide for your short-stay travel here in Stockholm, Sweden.

2

History of Sweden

For 2000 years (8000 B.C. to 6000 B.C.), the land that is now Sweden was the main hunting, gathering and fishing grounds for ancient people who used simple stone tools. Numerous artifacts that were used in the Nordic region during the Bronze Age had been found all over the country, with some even dating as far back as 1800 B.C. This marks the beginning of Sweden's history.

Fast forward to more than a thousand years later, in 500 B.C., when the land dwellers had settled in the area, and agriculture became the prominent backbone of the society. Stone tools were phased out, and iron tools replaced them quickly.

The Viking Age of Sweden didn't happen until much later, around 800 A.D. to 1050 A.D., when expeditions started moving towards the east. Traders traveled to the Baltic coast, with some even reaching as far out as the rivers of what is now the territory of Russia. Thievery and plunder were prominent during this era, when the region was yet to be introduced to religion.

The spread of religion and Christianity did not happen until the 9th century when a man named Ansgar came to the country with a mission to convert Vikings to believers. For two centuries, citizens fought back and restrained from religion, and it was not until the 11th century that Christianity successfully and widely influenced the region.

Around this time, the previously segregated provinces in the region were also combined into one territory. However, only in 1280 did King Magnus Ladulås authorized the establishment of noble families, marking the early roots of the monarchy in Sweden.

Economy and trade boomed during the first half of 14th century when German traders (called the Hanseatic League) brought goods and services to Sweden. However, the impressive and continuous rise of economy suddenly took a hit when the Black Death plagued the country in 1350. Both economy and population took a steep decline during this devastating time.

It was also during the fourteenth century that the Kalmar Union was established in Scandinavia. Denmark, Norway, and Sweden were congregated under Danish Queen Margareta's rule in 1389. From the late 14th century to the early 16th century, however, the Kalmar Union brewed internal conflicts between the three nations, and by 1520, the problem had gone out of hand when 80 members of the Swedish noble family were sentenced to die at the inauguration of Kristian II, then King of the Union. This event was later referred in history as the Stockholm Bloodbath.

A year later, Gustav Vasa, a member of the Swedish noble family, led the rebellion against the King of the Union. Kristian II was killed during the battle, and Gustav Vasa was then proclaimed King of Sweden, two years after the rebellion began.

Gustav Vasa reigned Sweden from 1523 to 1560. This is referred to as the Vasa Period in Sweden's history. During his reign as King, the crown took the church, and the monarchy was officially established as the way of governance in the country.

The 1600s was a great century for Sweden. They won several wars, including their victory against Denmark in the Thirty Years' War, and they also accumulated quite a few territories in Europe, including some provinces in the northernmost regions of Germany. They even had a small colony in present-day Delaware in the United States. The Baltic republics were also under Sweden's command. And, after proclamations of peace (of Westphalia in 1648 and of Roskilde in 1658) between Sweden and Denmark, this nation was considered one of the (if not the) greatest monarchy in the entire continent.

However, its prominently agrarian economy failed its ability to stay in power. After the Great Northern War of the early 1700s, Sweden lost its territories on the other side of the Baltic Sea. It lost again during the Napoleonic Wars, and had to surrender Finland to Russia, which was its last colony during this era.

In 1810, a French marshal Jean Baptiste Bernadotte was named heir to the crown. Four years later, he was successful in absorbing Norway into Sweden's regime. However, almost a century later, the two countries had a lot of internal disagreements that, ultimately, led them to part ways.

The 18th and 19th centuries marked a further decline in the country's economy and population. After its great loss in the Napoleonic Wars, the parliament decided to abolish the governmental rule of the Royal Family, but its trade and commerce were not at all helped by their decision to overhaul the government system. Citizens moved out of the country, and those who remained were still earning their wages through farming.

It was not until after World War II that Sweden experienced a rapid growth. In fact, its growing industrialism post-war made it one of Europe's fastest growing countries during this time.

Today, Sweden remains a beautiful country that has rich culture, art, and history.

3

Travel Season and Weather

Stockholm, Sweden is best visited during the summer. Although hotel rates and airfares may get a lot more expensive during this season, the city is a lot livelier and more vibrant than the rest of the year. Daylight can last for 24 hours during the summer months, giving you more time to explore the history, culture, and arts of Stockholm. The temperature in the warm season range between 68 and 71 degrees Fahrenheit during the day, and can drop to 10 to 20 degrees Fahrenheit at night.

However, if you are more interested in watching a few winter sports during your stay in the city, then it is best to visit around December to February. Less people travel to Stockholm during these months, which means the city is not as crowded as it is in the summer. You will find public transportation a lot easier during the winter, and hotels are not as booked as they are when the tourism in the city is at its peak.

If you want to learn more about the city's travel season and weather, below is a more detailed description of what you can expect for each month of the year in Stockholm.

January

January is the middle of winter in Stockholm, Sweden. You can enjoy many winter activities, as detailed in Chapter 12 of this travel guide. Also, January is when hotel rates and airfares get a lot cheaper. The holidays are over, so there are fewer tourists and smaller crowds. In other words, if you visit the city in January, you can experience Stockholm when it's relatively peaceful and quiet.

February

February is the month of winter sports. People come to watch and participate in winter sports including skiing, sledding, and snowboarding. You can also rent snowmobiles and ride through the snow. And though February is the coldest month of the year in Stockholm, the almost freezing temperature is worth it because of the frequent view of the Northern Lights.

Aside from the winter sports, February is the month of the Vikingarännet, or the Viking Run. The Vikingarännet is an ice-skating race event. Its course runs through Stockholm and Uppsala, which is another city in Sweden 44 miles north of its capital.

March

Days start to get longer and warmer in Stockholm during March. The winter slowly transitions into the beautiful green landscape that the city has. It is also during this month that the annual Vildmarksmässan, or Wildlife Fair, is held. The Wildlife Fair is an outdoor show with lots of different sporting events and activities.

The temperature in March is still pretty cold, ranging between 20 to 30 degrees Fahrenheit. Airfares and hotel rates will start to go up at the beginning of spring, but they are still a lot cheaper than they are during the summer.

April

April is your last chance to see the Northern Lights. It usually appears until late April, before it disappears for the rest of the year once again. April is also the month of Walpurgisnacht, or the Walpurgis Night, which is the eve of Saint Walpurga's feast day. During the Walpurgis Night, people have bonfires and dances on the streets, singing traditional spring folk songs loudly to ward off evil spirits.

May

Spring blooms in full during May. Parks and attractions open up to welcome both locals and tourists. There are also a lot of activities in Stockholm during this month. One of them is the Gärdesloppet, or the Gärde Race, which is a racing event for 1920s cars.

June

June is the beginning of summer in Stockholm. It marks the upward trajectory of the city's tourism as well. People from all over the world visit Stockholm because of its open-air events and attractions. They also stay for the midnight sun, a natural occurrence where the sun remains visible in the sky even at midnight. During this time, there is pretty much daylight for 24 hours, given that the weather conditions remain fair. This makes it a good time to explore the city and soak in its beauty. It is also when Scandinavians celebrate the Midsummer Festival, or the festival of the summer solstice.

Moreover, Smaka På Stockholm, or "A Taste of Stockholm", happens in June. It is an annual food festival in the city that attracts more than 350 thousand visitors from all over Sweden, Europe and the world.

July

July is usually the warmest month of the city. It also means that Stockholm is most crowded during this time of the year. Aside from the breathtaking view, the historical landmarks, and the countless museums and art galleries in the city, people come to Stockholm also for the largest Pride Parade in Scandinavia. Since it first began in 1998, participants and supporters have grown dramatically in Stockholm. In fact, in 2014, 60 thousand people came to participate and a whopping 600 thousand more followed the parade on the streets.

August

Because it is the last month of summer in Stockholm, hotel rates and airfare are still pretty expensive during August. But don't get disheartened; there are still a lot of things you can do in Stockholm to make your visit worthwhile. One of the most awaited events during August is Propaganda, a music festival arranged to highlight both established and upcoming musicians from Sweden and the rest of Europe. It is open to audiences aged 13 years and above. However, in order to get to the bar area, you must be at least 18 years old.

September

September is when Stockholm starts to get quieter. Its mild temperature makes it a good time to visit the city if you want to avoid crowds. Hotel rates and airfares also start to dwindle, averaging at $30 a night for a 3-star hotel.

Many events also happen during September. One of them is the Stockholm Beer and Whiskey Festival, which is usually held late September until early October. During this festival, you can attend several liquor and beer tastings and master classes.

Tjejmilen, or Ladies' Mile, is another event that is held in September. It is the largest sporting event for women in all of Sweden. Annually, it attracts more than 30 thousand participants from all over the country and the continent, and it happens usually at the beginning of the month.

Lastly, the Stockholm Half-Marathon is held usually in the first or second week of September. It has a 21.1-kilometer course (about 13 miles) that runs through some of the best tourist spots in Stockholm.

October

Prices continue to drop in October, but the weather is still good for travel. The temperature averages at about 50 degrees Fahrenheit during this month. Fewer people also visit during October, and so, if you have a small budget and a fear of big crowds, October is a lovely time to visit the city.

November

Ski resorts in Stockholm begin to open at the start of winter, which is November. Winter activities and sports become an attraction for tourists who love spending time in the snow. It is the best time to come to Stockholm if you want to experience the city in winter but are not willing to pay the expensive holiday rates during December.

December

If you wish to know what a Scandinavian Christmas is like, then you should obviously come to Stockholm in December. Prices may hike up a lot, but it will be worth the cost just to see the Northern Lights in the sky. You can also enjoy the holiday season by doing some winter activities such as skiing and sledding. And for a better picture of what you can do during the winter in Stockholm, make sure to read Chapter 12 of this book.

4

Transportation Options

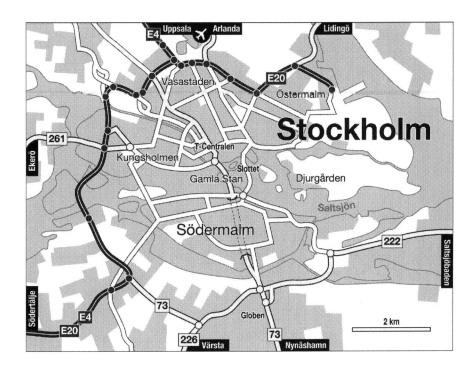

Stockholm Map
https://goo.gl/maps/j16nVHzNsRy

Airports

Stockholm has three major airports: the Stockholm Arlanda Airport, the Bromma Stockholm Airport, and the Stockholm Skavsta Airport (also known as the Nyköping Airport). You can also get to Stockholm from the Stockholm Västerås Airport (also known as the Hässlö Flygplats), which is located in the city of Västerås, about 68.5 miles west of Stockholm.

Stockholm Arlanda Airport Website
http://www.swedavia.com/arlanda/#gref
Stockholm Arlanda Airport Map
https://goo.gl/maps/e5w3Acvr3QQ2
Phone:+46 10 109 10 00

Bromma Stockholm Airport Website
http://www.swedavia.com/bromma/#gref
Bromma Stockholm Airport Map
https://goo.gl/maps/5J3d9hqVefn
Phone:+46 10 109 40 00

Stockholm Skavsta Airport Website
http://www.skavsta.se/en/
Stockholm Skavsta Airport Map
https://goo.gl/maps/4N8NRXztZN82
Phone:+46 155 28 04 00

Stockholm Västerås Airport Website
http://www.vst.nu/engelska-sidor/vasteras-airport.html
Stockholm Västerås Airport Map
https://goo.gl/maps/ds1vmM1e23k
Phone:+46 21 80 56 00

How to Get to Stockholm's City Center from These Airports

You have three options on how to get to the city center of Stockholm from the

- Arlanda Express Train: Located just below the arrival terminals, the Arlanda Express Train will take you to the city center in the fastest time. Trains leave every 15 minutes, and travel time will take only about 20 minutes.

Arlanda Express Train Website
https://www.arlandaexpress.com/contact.aspx
Phone:+46 771 720 200

- **Flygbussarna Airport Coaches**

Flygbussarna Airport Coaches Website
http://www.flygbussarna.se/en
Phone:0771-51 52 52
- **Train Station**

Arlanda Central Station Map
https://goo.gl/maps/dbJMqT1CM382

Transportation from the Bromma Stockholm Airport
- Flygbussarna Airport Coaches: Just like at the Stockholm Arlanda Airport, Flygbussarna Airport Coaches operate on these three other airports in Stockholm. Travel time to the city center from the Bromma Stockholm Airport is 20 minutes, while that from the Stockholm Skavsta Airport or the Stockholm Västerås Airport is

80 minutes. Departure times of the Flygbussarna Airport Coaches vary, depending on the departure and arrival schedules in these three airports.

Flygbussarna Airport Coaches Website
http://www.flygbussarna.se/en/customer-services
Phone: 0771-51 52 52
00 46 771 51 52 52

· If you do not opt to travel via bus or train, you can always take a cab from the Stockholm Arlanda Airport and the Bromma Stockholm Airport. Depending on the time of the day, travel from the Stockholm Arlanda Airport to the city center via taxi takes about 40 minutes, while travel from the Bromma Stockholm Airport to the city center via taxi takes about 15 minutes.

Note, also, that cab fares in Sweden are not regulated. Therefore, different cab companies may have different fare rates. To make sure your cab driver does not scam you, Stockholm's official website suggests that you only take a ride on cabs operating under Taxi 020, Taxi Kurir, and Taxi Stockholm. These taxi firms are well-established in Stockholm because of their good services and reasonable prices. They also accept credit card payments.

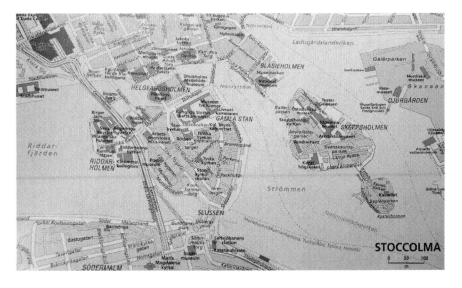

Public Transportation

The Stockholm Public Transport (SL) controls the city's public transportation system. It has two types of tickets, both of which are used in all of SL's public transportation services.

Public Transportation Website
http://sl.se/en/
Metro 2
https://www.mtr.com.hk/en/corporate/consultancy/
stockholmmetro.html

(1)Zone tickets are used for short trips. They only last for an hour after they are stamped, but you can use them if you plan to transfer into another form of public transport. You can purchase zone tickets as cash tickets (available at train and bus stations, and also from conductors), pre-paid tickets (single units and 16-unit slips available at resellers, 16-unit slips also available at train and bus stations), text message tickets (via mobile purchase, and is valid for 15 more minutes, as margin for the time of purchase), and vending machine tickets (via ticket machines in select bus and train stations, paid with card or coins).

(2)Travel cards are suggested for tourists who plan to go around the city a lot. They can last for 24 hours to up to a year, depending on which type you purchase. They are valid across SL zones, and can be bought in SL centers around Stockholm.

If you're planning to use zone tickets instead of buying a travel card during your stay in Stockholm, then you should know about SL's zone system. Basically, SL divided the city in three zones, with Zone A covering the city center and most of the inner suburbs, Zone B covering the area between Zones A and C, and Zone C covering most of the outer suburbs.

If you want to travel through these zones, you will need different zone tickets. You will also need additional tickets if you want to travel to zones outside the border of Stockholm (for example in Bålsta or Gnesta). The latter holds the case even if you purchased a travel card.

For your short-stay travel, it is suggested that you purchase a 3-day travel card. It is priced at about $28 for people between 20 and 65 years old. If you are younger or older than those age restrictions, you will only have to pay about $17.

For zone tickets, the following is a breakdown of prices. Note: Discounted prices, again, are for people younger than 20 years old and older than 65 years old.

(1)Cash Tickets
Regular price per unit: $3.00
Discounted price per unit $2.00

(2)Pre-paid Tickets
Regular price per unit: $2.25
Discounted price per unit: $1.50

Regular price per 16 units: $23.75
Discounted price per 16 units: $13.00

(3)Text Message Tickets and Vending Machine Tickets
Regular price for 1 zone: $4.25
Discounted price for 1 zone: $2.50
Regular price for 2 zones: $6.50
Discounted price for 2 zones: $3.50
Regular price for 3 zones: $8.50
Discounted price for 3 zones. $4.75

Experience Stockholm on a Bicycle

One of the best ways to experience Stockholm is on a bike.You can rent a bicycle and ride around the bike paths all over the city.
Bicycle Website
http://www.rentabike.se/

Bicycle Map
https://goo.gl/maps/pLr3Vy3yKyq
Phone: +46 8 660 79 59

5

Best Affordable Hotels

Traveling to Sweden does not have to be expensive. For your short-stay travel in Stockholm, here are the top 5 affordable hotels around the area.

Connect Hotel Stockholm

Location: Alströmergatan 41, 112 47 Stockholm, Sweden
Tel:+46 8 441 02 20
Starting Price: $29.25
Rating: 3 Stars

From the Connect Hotel Stockholm in Götalandsvägen, it only takes two train stops via the Pendeltág train for you to get to the center of the city. From there, you can explore Stockholm's famous landmarks, such as the Riddarholmskyrkan, which is the oldest building in the Stockholm. The hotel has 95 modern-styled rooms, and you can choose whether you want to have bunk beds with shared bathrooms or double beds with a private bath. You can also find a lounge, a restaurant, and a bar/café inside the hotel.

Connect Hotel Stockholm Website
http://connecthotels.se/en/
Connect Hotel Stockholm Map
https://goo.gl/maps/HiBsRHacVCv

Rex Petit Hotel
Location: Luntmakargatan 73, 113 51 Stockholm, Sweden
Tel:+46 8 23 66 99
Starting Price: $35
Rating: 2 Stars

If you like to discover Stockholm's vibrant media and music scene, then the Rex Petit Hotel is the best accommodation for you. Located in the city center in the Vasastaden district, it is only a short walk away from famous Stockholm musical landmarks such as the Opera House. The streets around the hotel are also famous for its nightlife. You can find a lot of restaurants, bars, cafés, and clubs in the area.

The Rex Petit Hotel is relatively small compared to the other hotels on this list. With only 22 rooms, you can choose between bunk beds that come with private bathrooms or double beds that have communal bathrooms.

Rex Petit Hotel Website
http://rexpetit.se/en/Rex_petit
Rex Petit Hotel Map
https://goo.gl/maps/CdzbkoVWBYM2

Scandic Ariadne

Location: Södra Kajen 37, 115 74 Stockholm, Sweden
Tel:+46 8 517 386 00
Starting Price: $43.50
Rating: 3 Stars

The Scandic Ariadne has a simple yet cozy aesthetic that makes travelers feel at home. It has 283 private bedrooms with en suite bathrooms, as well as a few superior, more spacious bedrooms that feature a mini bar.

The hotel also has a restaurant (the Mistral) and a bar (the Sky Bar) within its premises. Both of these venues have terrific views of Stockholm; from the Mistral, you can sit on the terrace that overlooks the harbor, and from the Sky Bar, you have a view of the city skyline.

The Stockholm Central Station is just 6 minutes away from the Gärdet metro station, which is a 15-minute walk away from the hotel. But if you will rather take the bus to get to other places in the city, the Ropsten metro station is also close by.

Scandic Ariadne Website
https://www.scandichotels.se/hotell/sverige/
stockholm/scandic-ariadne

Scandic Ariadne Map
https://goo.gl/maps/CfoGdAWckMS2

Scandic Bromma
Location: Brommaplan, 168 76 Stockholm, Sweden
Tel:+46 8 517 341 00
Starting Price: $50
Rating: 2 Stars

You can choose from the Scandic Bromna's 144 cozy private bedrooms. All of their units come with an en suite bathroom and a shower.

Stockholm landmarks that are close to the Scandic Bromna include the breathtaking Drottningholm Palace, which has been declared a UNESCO Heritage Site. This tourist spot and the Stockholm Airport are just about 2 miles away from the hotel. You can also reach the city center in about twenty minutes by taking the bus.

Scandic Bromma Website
https://www.scandichotels.se/hotell/sverige/stockholm/scandic-bromma
Scandic Bromma Map
https://goo.gl/maps/rqHhWZgH5fR2

Scandic Park
Location: Karlavägen 43, 102 46 Stockholm, Sweden
Tel:+46 8 517 348 00
Starting Price: $52.25
Rating: 3 Stars

The Scandic Park is conveniently located in the center of Stockholm. It has 201 private bedrooms that come with en suite baths. From the hotel, you can have a view of the beautiful Humlegården Park, which is a major park in the district. In the Humlegården Park, you will find the Royal Library and a statue of Linnaeus (Carl von Linné), who is a famous Swedish scientist. The Stockholm Stadium is also a short distance away, while the Stadion metro stop is a 3-minute walking distance from the hotel.

Scandic Park Website
https://www.scandichotels.se/hotell/sverige/stockholm/scandic-park
Scandic Park Map
https://goo.gl/maps/8Ay6rekK7qF2

6

Best Restaurants

An important part of any culture is its food, and what better way to get to know Stockholm than to experience its delicious cuisine. Here are the top 5 restaurants in the city.

Gro

Location: Sankt Eriksgatan 67, 113 32 Stockholm, Sweden
Opening Hours: 5:30 P.M. to 11:00 P.M. Tuesday – Saturday
Phone:+46 8 643 42 22
Price Range: $58.75 for a four-course meal

If you are especially fond of eating vegetables (or in Swedish, grönsaker, which means "green things"), then Gro is the restaurant for you. Here, head chefs Henrik Norén and Magnus Villnow present locally grown vegetables and ingredients in an elevated manner. One of their specialty dishes uses cauliflower in several unique ways—puréed, roasted, pickled, and raw—and you can enjoy such creative dishes like this one at Gro every day during lunch. (Unfortunately, the restaurant is currently serving dinner every Thursday only.)

Gro Website
http://grorestaurang.se/
Gro Map
https://goo.gl/maps/DTFGTzukvwM2

Lilla Ego

Location: Västmannagatan 69, 113 26 Stockholm, Sweden
Opening Hours: 5:00 P.M. to 11:00 P.M. Tuesday – Saturday
Phone:+46 8 27 44 55
Price Range: $16.50 to $37.75

Lilla Ego may the priciest restaurant on this list, but it is absolutely worth it. Head chef Tom Sjöstedt and his business partner Daniel Räms were both awarded Chef of the Year and have now come together to create their own culinary masterpieces. In fact, the restaurant has risen in popularity since it opened on November of 2013. In order to secure a table at this famous yet unpretentious restaurant, you will have to book three months in advance.

Lilla Ego Website
http://www.lillaego.com/
Lilla Ego Map
https://goo.gl/maps/tAa9raEH4xB2

Nook

Location: Åsögatan 176, 116 32 Stockholm, Sweden
Opening Hours: 5:00 P.M. to 11:00 P.M. Tuesday – Saturday
Bar is open until 1:00 A.M. except on Tuesdays
Phone:+46 8 702 12 22
Price Range: $13 to $31.25

If you suddenly crave for a little Swedish and Asian fusion while in Stockholm, then you should definitely check out Nook. Head chef Claes Grännsjö was actually born in Korea, and so his menu items are inspired heavily by this country's cuisine. In Nook's menu, you will find traditional Swedish dishes like Torskrygg (cod) with ägg (egg), gröna ärtor (green peas), parmesan, and sardeller (sardines), along with unique Korean food items such as blood sausage.

Nook Website
http://nookrestaurang.se/
Nook Map
https://goo.gl/maps/XTQpjrkEUqx

Nytorget 6

Location: Nytorget 6, 116 40 Stockholm, Sweden
Opening Hours: 7:30 A.M. to 12:00 A.M. Monday – Tuesday
7:30 A.M. to 1:00 A.M. Wednesday – Friday
10:00 A.M. to 1:00 A.M. Saturday
10:00 A.M. to 12:00 A.M. Sunday
Phone:+46 8 640 96 55
Price Range: $18.25 to $27.75 (for main courses on their evening menu)

Its comfort foos and cozy atmosphere make Nytorget 6 such a delight to its customers. Because its main courses are priced very affordably, people are always coming back to enjoy what the restaurant has to offer. One of its most popular dishes is the råraka, a grated potato pancake cooked to a crisp and served with bleak roe, red onions, and sour cream. You can try Nytorget 6's råraka dish, or you can order their premium cut steak, served with chips, and drizzled with a little bit of béarnaise sauce.

Nytorget 6 Website

http://www.nytorget6.com/

Nytorget 6 Map

https://goo.gl/maps/iBzFT9EDony

Speceriet

Location: Artillerigatan 14, 114 51 Stockholm, Sweden

Opening Hours: 5:00 P.M. to 11:00 P.M. Monday and Saturday

11:30 A.M. to 2:00 P.M. and 5:00 P.M. to 11 P.M. Tuesday – Friday

Phone:+46 8 662 30 60

Price Range: Currently not listed on their website

Speceriet is located in the wealthy district of Östermalm in Stockholm, yet it's delicious food items have very affordable prices. It is no wonder why this quaint, little restaurant is popular to both locals and tourists, especially because its two head chefs, Jacob Holmström and Anton Bjuhr, are experienced in their fine-dining, Michelin-starred restaurant called Gastrologik. If you happen to come by the Östermalm district in Stockholm, make sure to try out Speceriet's fried pickled salmon, served on a crispbread with potatoes and caper mayonnaise.

Speceriet Website

http://speceriet.se/?lang=en

Speceriet Map

https://goo.gl/maps/dA3c9DFdJi62

7

Most Famous Landmarks

Learning about Stockholm's history and culture is as easy as visiting its most famous landmarks. Here are the 5 most famous landmarks in Sweden's capital. (Note: Admission fees are rounded up to the nearest dollar value.)

The City Hall
Location: Hantverkargatan 1, 111 52 Stockholm, Sweden
Opening Hours: 8:00 A.M. to 4:30 P.M. Weekdays
Admission Fees: $8.25 to $11.75

Stockholm's City Hall has always been a tourist attraction. At the peak of its 348-foot tower is a spire that holds the national coat of arms of Sweden, the golden Three Crowns. Designed by architect Ragnar Östberg, the building is considered a beacon of Sweden's national romanticism in architecture.

Today, the City Hall is home to the great Nobel banquet, a celebration that honors outstanding individuals from their respective fields. Offices and session halls can also be found behind the classic façade, where Stockholm's officials and politicians conduct their businesses.
The City Hall Map
https://goo.gl/maps/JUifkQY6Su42

Drottningholm Palace
Location: 178 02 Drottningholm, Stockholm, Sweden
Opening Hours: 10:00 A.M. to 4:30 P.M. Daily

Admission Fees: $14

Part of UNESCO's World Heritage List, the Drottningholm Palace is the current home of Sweden's Royal Majesties, the King and the Queen, and the rest of the Royal family. It was built in the 1600s and designed by architect Nicodemus Tessin the Elder, who was chosen by then Queen Hedvig Eleonora to lead the project. The south wing of the palace is reserved for the Majesties' residences, but the rest of the structure and the grounds are open to tourists and visitors. Inside the Drottningholm Palace, you will find the Museum De Vries, which is an outstanding collection of bronze sculptures created by Dutch artist Adriaen de Vrie in the 1700s, and the Royal Chapel, which has been the venue of numerous Royal events since 1746.

Drottningholm Palace Website

http://goo.gl/pzioCk

Drottningholm Palace Map

https://goo.gl/maps/vNhVbJPwVNs

Gamla Stan

Location: Gamla Stan, Stockholm, Sweden
Opening Hours: None
Admission Fees: None

Stockholm was first founded in 1252, in the beautiful town of Gamla Stan. Today, the Old Town, as both locals and tourists know Gamla Stan, serves as a reminder of Sweden's rich history. It is the biggest and most well-preserved medieval town in the entire continent, and it attracts international visitors with its historical architecture, as well as its abundant museums, bars, cafés, restaurants, and shopping centers.

If you visit Gamla Stan, you will have the chance to walk through beautiful cobblestone roads that wind through golden buildings and structures. Take a detour at Sweden's oldest square, Stortorget, and its oldest street, Köpmangatan. Around this area, you will also find the Stockholm Cathedral (Sweden's national church), the Royal Palace, and the Nobel Museum.

Gamla Stan Map
https://goo.gl/maps/9Ak25gj1DCq

Kungliga Operan
Location: Gustav Adolfs torg 2, 103 22 Stockholm, Sweden
Opening Hours: Varies between shows
Admission Fees: Varies between shows
Phone:+46 8 791 44 00

The Kungliga Operan or the Royal Swedish Opera hosts countless productions of theater, dance and music every year. Opening its door to the public in the late 1700s, the Kungliga Operan is Sweden's national stage. Even if you're not planning to see ballet or the opera during your stay in Stockholm, still make some time to visit the opera house and appreciate its lavishly ornate design. After all, it is big part of Stockholm and Sweden's culture and art.

Kungliga Operan Website
http://www.operan.se/
Kungliga Operan Map
https://goo.gl/maps/sMivfRf7Py12

Skansen Open-Air Museum

Location: Djurgårdsslätten 49-51, 115 21 Stockholm, Sweden
Opening Hours: Varies widely, see website for details (
Admission Fees: $7 to $21

Artur Hazelius founded Skansen, the first ever open-air museum in the world, in 1891. At Skansen, you will learn about the Swedish life through the centuries. You can also meet local Nordic animals, as well as enjoy annual festivities like St. Lucia's Day, which is held on December.

Skansen Open-Air Museum Website
http://www.skansen.se/en/kategori/english
Skansen Open-Air Museum Map
https://goo.gl/maps/bXpLcjzeJSU2

8

Must-Visit Museums

Art is an important part of any country or city's culture. Here are 5 museums in Stockholm you definitely should not miss. (Note: Museums listed in this chapter have free admissions unless noted otherwise.)

Medeltidsmuseet
Location: Strömparrterren 3, 111 30 Stockholm, Sweden
Opening Hours: 12:00 P.M. to 5:00 P.M. Tuesday, Thursday – Sunday
12:00 P.M. to 8:00 P.M. Wednesday

If you want to take a glimpse of Sweden's history, then you should visit the Medeltidsmuseet or the Medieval Museum in Stockholm. In their underground exhibition, you will find excavations of medieval town walls built in the 16th century. They also have an archaeological display of a market square, a church, and a council hall, all three of which are important parts of the country's medieval civilization.
Medeltidsmuseet Website
http://medeltidsmuseet.stockholm.se/in-english/
Medeltidsmuseet Map
https://goo.gl/maps/DXY449CDW8T2

Moderna Museet
Location: Exercisplan 4, Skeppsholmen, Stockholm, Sweden

Opening Hours: 10:00 A.M. to 8:00 P.M. Tuesday
10:00 A.M. to 6:00 P.M. Wednesday – Sunday

The Moderna Museet or the Modern Museum is probably the most famous museum in Stockholm. First opening its doors to the public in 1958, the Moderna Museet is home to contemporary artists who want to express their unique creativity.
Moderna Museet Website
http://www.modernamuseet.se/stockholm/en/
Moderna Museet Map
https://goo.gl/maps/ome9CmGGKs42

Nobel Museet
Location: Stortorget 2, 103 16 Stockholm, Sweden
Opening Hours: 9:00 A.M. to 8:00 P.M. Daily

The Nobel Museet was opened in 2001 as a center of knowledge and interest. It honors the life of Alfred Nobel, founder of the Nobel Prize, as well as the achievements of the Nobel Laureates. Its exhibitions range from science to art to design, and it even houses literary masterpieces such as that of Romanian-born German author Herta Müller.

Note: Free admission in the Nobel Museet is only on Tuesdays, from 5:00 P.M. to 8:00 P.M. Regular admission costs $12 for adults and $8 for students and senior citizens. Children up to 18 years old are admitted free.

Nobel Museet Website
http://www.nobelmuseum.se/
Nobel Museet Map
https://goo.gl/maps/Vdb5Ms5VvdT2

Vasa Museet

Location: Galärvarvsvägen 14, 115 21 Stockholm, Sweden
Opening Hours: June to August 8:30 A.M. to 6:00 P.M. Daily
September to May 10:00 A.M. to 5:00 P.M. Daily (except Wednesdays, 10:00 A.M. to 8:00 P.M.

Vasa was a real warship in the 17th century that sunk just minutes after leaving shore, and the Vasa Museet is where you can learn more about this historical catastrophe. There are exhibits detailing why Vasa was considered the great machine of war before it sank, what investigation followed the tragedy, and how the ship was salvaged so that it could continue to serve as a reminder of the country's past.

Note: Admission is only free for children up to 18 years old. The admission fee is $15.25 for adults and $12 for students.

Vasa Museet Website

http://www.vasamuseet.se/en

Vasa Museet Map

https://goo.gl/maps/gmBZ1R9VJRz

Arkitektur-och Designcentrum Skeppsholmen (ArkDes)

Location: Exercisplan 4, 111 49 Stockholm, Sweden

Opening Hours: 10:00 A.M. to 8:00 P.M. Tuesday

10:00 A.M. to 6:00 P.M. Wednesday – Sunday

Arkitektur-och Designcentrum Skeppsholmen, or ArkDes, is a national museum focusing on architecture and design. First founded in 1962, it exhibits the work of over 500 architects from all over Europe and the world. Its library is the home of more than 24 thousand books, and it archives architectural and design journals from the 1930s to the present time.

    Arkitektur-och Designcentrum Skeppsholmen Website
http://www.arkdes.se/
Arkitektur-och Designcentrum Skeppsholmen Map
https://goo.gl/maps/K7cMDkSFik32

9

Must-Visit Art Galleries

If you still want to soak yourself with Swedish art and culture after visiting the museums from the last chapter, then these 5 art galleries are a must-visit for you.

Andréhn-Schiptjenko

Location: 2nd Floor, Hudiksvallsgatan 8, 113 30 Stockholm, Sweden
Opening Hours: 11:00 A.M. to 7:00 P.M. Thursday
11:00 A.M. to 4:00 P.M. Friday – Sunday
Admission Fees: None

Andréhn-Schiptjenko is a gallery that aims to influence future movements in art. With exhibitions from Scandinavian artists like Annika Larsson and Annika von Hausswolff, its growing popularity opened opportunities for bigger projects, including its participation in international art fairs in China, Mexico, and America. If you are in the mood for some contemporary art, then definitely pay Andréhn-Schiptjenko a visit during your stay in Stockholm.
Andréhn-Schiptjenko Website
http://www.andrehn-schiptjenko.com/
Andréhn-Schiptjenko Map
https://goo.gl/maps/aEjVUUvgr2u

Färgfabriken
Location: Lövholmsbrinken 1, 117 43 Stockholm, Sweden
Opening Hours: 11:00 A.M. to 6:00 P.M. Tuesday – Friday
12:00 P.M. to 4:00 P.M. Saturday
Admission Fees: $7 Regular Admission
$6 Students and Senior Citizens
Free for children up to 18 years old

Färgfabriken first opened in 1995, and it has since served as an art gallery for cultural and contemporary works of architecture, art, and urban design. Its main goal is to bring creativity from the world to Stockholm, and in effect, Färgfabriken to the rest of the world. Färgfabriken is the art gallery for people who want to immerse themselves in a global culture while visiting Stockholm. It is a good place to know how the city and Sweden react to globalization.
Färgfabriken Website

https://www.facebook.com/fargfabriken/
Färgfabriken Map
https://goo.gl/maps/Gpg7HfQhVn52

Fotografiska
Location: Stadsgårdshamnen 22, 116 45 Stockholm, Sweden
Opening Hours: 9:00 A.M. to 11:00 P.M. Sunday – Wednesday
9:00 A.M. to 1:00 A.M. Thursday – Saturday
Admission Fees: $14 Regular Admission
$10.50 Students and Senior Citizens
Free for children up to 12 years old

If photography is more up your alley, then Fotografiska is where you should go. This 2500-square-meter art gallery annually hosts 4 major and 15 to 20 minor exhibits. It features photographers from all over the world, and welcomes more than 500 thousand visitors each year. Because of the diversity of its artists, you should expect unique exhibitions that will not only entertain but will also arouse curiosity, creativity, and controversy. Fotografiska promises a worthwhile visit that will change your perspective of the world when you leave this art gallery.
Fotografiska Website
http://fotografiska.eu/en/
Fotografiska Map
https://goo.gl/maps/4JJnh4ECg7v

Galleri Charlotte Lund
Location: 6th Floor, Kungstensgatan 23, 113 57 Stockholm, Sweden
Opening Hours: 12:00 P.M. to 6:00 P.M. Tuesday – Friday
12:00 P.M. to 4:00 P.M. Saturday
Admission Fees: Currently not listed

Charlotte Lund founded the Galleri Charlotte Lund in 1993 with the purpose of opening visitors' eyes to the beauty and sophistication of contemporary art. This art gallery features established and upcoming Swedish artists at the same time. Unlike Fotografiska, Galleri Charlotte Lund is more rounded when it comes to the form of art. Here, you will find paintings, sketches, photographs, sculptures, videos, and installations that will all steer your creative mind.

Galleri Charlotte Lund Website

http://www.gallericharlottelund.com/

Galleri Charlotte Lund Map

https://goo.gl/maps/dBFma9XtPkn

Liljevalchs

Location: Djurgårdsvägen 60, 115 21 Stockholm, Sweden

Opening Hours: 11:00 A.M. to 5:00 P.M. Tuesday – Sunday

Admission Fees: Currently not listed on their website

Liljevalchs is the first ever independent contemporary art gallery in Sweden. First opened in 1916, this beautiful public museum was designed by architect Carl Bergsten, who intended to invite nature within its space. It hosts four major exhibitions every year, and it mostly features artists who specialize in contemporary and trendy forms of art and design.

Liljevalchs Website

https://www.facebook.com/liljevalchs/

Liljevalchs Map

https://goo.gl/maps/MbSEp1QhMHu

10

Best Coffee Shops

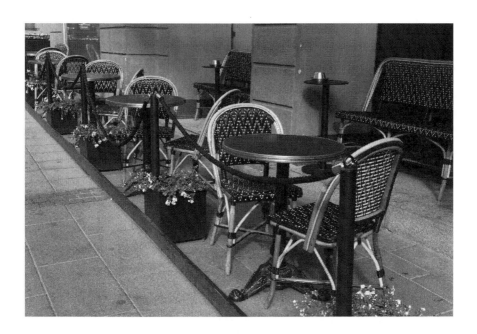

Aside from its rich art and history, Stockholm is best known for its coffee culture. Here in Stockholm, you will find numerous cafés that will satisfy your coffee craving. But to make your short travel a lot easier, this chapter has listed 5 of Stockholm's best coffee shops just for you. (Note: Price ranges listed on this chapter cover food items on the menu. Expect prices of coffee to be lower or within the range.)

Café Pascal
Location: 29C Östgötagatan, 116 25 Stockholm, Sweden
Opening Hours: 7:00 A.M. to 7:00 P.M. Monday – Thursday
7:00 A.M. to 6:00 P.M. Friday
9:00 A.M. to 6:00 P.M. Weekdays
Price Range: Currently not listed on their website

Rustic and industrial with a few modern touches, Café Pascal has a mid-century modern yet cozy ambiance that will make you feel at home. Its bright and airy space, as well as its good food and delicious coffee, make it one of the most visited coffee shops in Stockholm. Here, you can taste their signature bread and pastries while sipping a cup of their freshly brewed and slowly roasted fika. If you are looking for something to eat for lunch, you can also try their sandwiches and salads.

Café Pascal Website
http://cafepascal.se/
Café Pascal Map
https://goo.gl/maps/H1GKTjSUqC62

Coffice
Location: 29C Östgötagatan, 116 25 Stockholm, Sweden
Opening Hours: 7:45 A.M. to 6:00 P.M. Weekdays
10:00 A.M. to 6:00 P.M. Saturday
10:00 A.M. to 5:00 P.M. Saturday
Price Range: Currently not listed on their website

Coffice takes coffee ingenuity to heart. Opening its innovative space in 2009, Coffice (C from café and Office from office) is a place where people can work and enjoy coffee at the same time. The idea behind this coffee shop is to create an urban space to promote the working culture for those who are tired of working in the office or at home. In fact, customers can become members if they want to work at Coffice regularly, and they are given their own spaces in the coffee shop.

So if you have a few emails to send while in Stockholm, why don't you try visiting Coffice for a little cup of coffee? And even if you are planning to leave all work back at home, their delicious food, and drinks are still worth your time.

Coffice Website
http://coffice.coop/en/
Coffice Map
https://goo.gl/maps/vubi7Swkaj72

Drop Coffee
Location: Wollmar Yxkullsgatan 10, 118 50 Stockholm, Sweden
Opening Hours: 8:00 A.M. to 5:00 P.M. Weekdays
10:00 A.M. to 5:00 P.M. Weekends
Price Range: Currently not listed on their website

Joana Alm and Stephen Leighton, owners of Drop Coffee Café and Drop Coffee Roasters, are both experts in the art of roasting and brewing coffee. In their coffee shop, they serve their best coffee products, as well as lunch and breakfast items that were all well-crafted and thought-out. Alm and Leighton train their baristas to always achieve the perfect combination of acidity and sweetness in their coffee products. During your visit in Stockholm, stop by the Drop Coffee Café to taste their food and drinks, and maybe take home some of their wonderful coffee beans as well.

Drop Coffee Website
http://www.dropcoffee.com/

Drop Coffee Map
https://goo.gl/maps/PJd1PkopW642

Kafé Esaias

Location: Drottninggatan 102, 111 60 Stockholm, Sweden
Opening Hours: 7:30 A.M. to 5:00 P.M. Weekdays
10:00 A.M. to 5:00 P.M. Weekends
Price Range: $7.75 to $19

Kafé Esaias does not only serve delicious coffee; they have a full breakfast and lunch menu, too. Some of their breakfast items include sandwiches, granola, and sourdough, while their lunch menu includes a variety of salads and sandwiches. On weekends, they also serve a big brunch meal that will surely make your tummy happy. Kafé Esaias is popular for its warm and cozy ambience, and if you like to munch on some delicious comfort food during your visit in Stockholm, then give this coffee shop a try.

Kafé Esaias Website
https://www.facebook.com/kafeesaias/
Kafé Esaias Map
https://goo.gl/maps/a1UbHg67rxP2

Vete-Katten

Location: Kungsgatan 55, 111 22 Stockholm, Sweden
Opening Hours: 7:30 A.M. to 10:00 P.M. Weekdays
9:30 A.M. to 7:00 P.M. Weekends
Price Range: $9.25 to $14

Breakfast, salads, sandwiches, buns, biscuits, pastries, wine, tea, and coffee—Vete-Katten has it all. Famous for its freshly brewed cups of fika, the classic and elegant coffee shop will satisfy every craving you may ever have while in Stockholm. In fact, it is one of the most visited cafés in the city, and it has grown exponentially since Ester Nordhammar first opened it in 1928. Today, head chef Johan Sandelin continues to serve Vete-Katten's customers with good food and delicious drinks. His numerous awards, including Pastry Chef of the Year that he has won in 2002, can prove his talent in gastronomy.

Vete-Katten Website
http://www.vetekatten.se/en/
Vete-Katten Map
https://goo.gl/maps/zS67Kfx5mHD2

11

Nightlife—Best Bars

When you have seen the sights and have been soaked in the culture of Stockholm during the day, you might want to take a break from history lessons and try having some fun. In this chapter, you will find ways to enjoy the city's nightlife with these 5 awesome bars.

Erlands
Location: Gästrikegatan 1, 113 62 Stockholm, Sweden
Opening Hours: 5:00 P.M. to 11:00 P.M. Monday – Thursday
4:00 P.M. to 12:00 A.M. Friday – Saturday
Price Range: Drink prices currently not listed on their website

Erland opened only in 2013, yet its vintage design and ambience will take you back to the 1930s. This bar is a good place to have a drink and unwind. You can enjoy live performances while eating their delicious menu items and drinking their wide range of cocktails and other beverages.

Erlands Website
https://www.facebook.com/ErlandsCocktails/
Erlands Map
https://goo.gl/maps/MhxNX722mUA2

Häktet
Location: Hornsgatan 82, 118 21 Stockholm, Sweden
Opening Hours: 5:00 P.M. to 12:00 A.M. Monday – Tuesday
5:00 P.M. to 1:00 A.M. Wednesday
5:00 P.M. to 3:00 A.M. Thursday – Saturday
Price Range: $5.25 to $60 (for regular drinks)

In English, Häktet literally means detention, which makes sense as a name for this hip bar in Stockholm because it was built on the grounds where a jail was once erect. Nowadays, Häktet means good wine and liquor. With its white range of spirits, you will surely find something that suits your taste. The price of drinks start as low as $5.25, but the bar also sells the finest champagne, like the 1996 Vueve Clicquot Magnum Rose, which is priced at about $610.

Häktet also has a food menu that features delicious starters, main courses, and desserts. Starters begin at $3.50 (per oyster), main courses begin at $26.50, and desserts begin at $6.50.

Häktet Website
https://www.facebook.com/haktet/
Häktet Map
https://goo.gl/maps/NRBfSgoowP72

Pharmarium
Location: Stortorget 7, 111 29 Stockholm, Sweden
Opening Hours: 6:00 P.M. to 2:00 A.M. Wednesday – Saturday
Price Range: $16.50 to $18.25

Inspired by the first pharmacy built in the city, Pharmarium gets a little scientific when making its drinks. It has concoctions like Tea + Therapy, where they combine different types of tea with Hendrick's gin. At Pharmarium, your palette will have a wonderful time experimenting with exotic combinations of liquor and other ingredients.

Pharmarium Website
http://pharmarium.se/
Pharmarium Map
https://goo.gl/maps/63pMUnsUsE22

Restaurang Aktiebolaget Kvarnen
Location: Tjärhovsgatan 4, 116 21 Stockholm, Sweden

Opening Hours: 11:00 A.M. to 1:00 A.M. Monday – Tuesday
11:00 A.M. to 3:00 A.M. Wednesday to Friday
12:00 P.M. to 3:00 A.M. Saturday
12:00 P.M. to 1:00 A.M. Sunday
Price Range: $6.50 to $23.35 (for regular drinks)

Restaurang Aktiebolaget Kvarnen, or simply Kvarnen, is one of the most popular bars in Stockholm. It has a tavern theme that pays homage to the year when it first opened, back in 1908. The atmosphere here is warm and lively, and it takes you back to the farmstead life that people lived in Sweden all those years ago. Kvarnen has many drink options, but its bestseller is the classic beer. You should also try their food and wine.

Restaurang Aktiebolaget Kvarnen Website
https://www.facebook.com/kvarnen.hospodske.dveri/
Restaurang Aktiebolaget Kvarnen Map
https://goo.gl/maps/ewoYdXCjnFn

Tweed
Location: Lilla Nygatan 5, 111 28 Stockholm, Sweden
Opening Hours: 5:00 P.M. to 12:00 A.M. Monday – Thursday
3:00 P.M. to 1:00 A.M. Friday
5:00 P.M. to 1:00 A.M. Saturday
Price Range: Currently not listed on the website

All aboard!—Tweed has a nautical theme that goes along well with their liquor and other alcohol products. Here at Tweed, you can have a nice drink, smoke a good Cuban, and eat some delicious food—just like the sailors back in the day did. Moreover, they sometimes have live performances that you can enjoy during your visit. Their snacks are priced as low as $4, while their main course items start at $20.56.

Tweed Website
http://start.leijontornet.se/
Tweed Map
https://goo.gl/maps/HZSfj3dAiuH2

12

Nightlife—Best Nightclubs

If drinking and dancing are more your thing, then a simple bar might not be enough. Here are 5 of the best places to dance the night away in Stockholm:

Göta Källare
Location: Folkungagatan 45, 118 26 Stockholm, Sweden
Opening Hours: 10:00 P.M. to 3:00 A.M. Wednesday, Friday – Saturday

If one dance floor isn't enough for you, then check out Göta Källare and its 2 dance floors. Divided into 2 levels, its almost 4000-square-foot dance floor is enough space for everyone to enjoy their techno beats and futuristic sounds. They have live DJs performing, so you know you will have a good time.

Göta Källare Website
http://gotakallare.com/site/
Göta Källare Map
https://goo.gl/maps/JgkjoGKKrcK2

Kåken
Location: Regeringsgatan 66, 111 39 Stockholm, Sweden
Opening Hours: 5:00 A.M. to 11:00 P.M. Monday – Thursday

4:00 A.M. to 12:00 A.M. Friday – Saturday

Kåken suits the more elegant and classy crowd. Its vintage interior will definitely bring you back to the 20s and 30s, but you will still have a really good time hanging out in this club.

Kåken Website
https://www.facebook.com/kakensthlm
Kåken Map
https://goo.gl/maps/5TpbGAYC1Bm

Restaurang Solidaritet
Location: Lästmakargatan 3, 111 44 Stockholm, Sweden
Opening Hours: 11:00 P.M. to 5:00 A.M. Wednesday – Saturday

Modern, trendy and fun—those are just some of the words that describe Restaurang Solidaritet. Aside from its crowded and energetic dance floor, and its great music from Swedish and international DJs, this club also has a refreshing menu of drinks that you will surely love.

Restaurang Solidaritet Website
https://www.facebook.com/SLDRTT/
Restaurang Solidaritet Map
https://goo.gl/maps/YZt3QFCTAPM2

Södra Bar
Location: Mosebacke Torg 1, 116 46 Stockholm
Opening Hours: 5:00 A.M. to 11:00 P.M. Monday – Thursday
4:00 A.M. to 12:00 A.M. Friday – Saturday

Another place with good drinks and great live acts is the Södra Bar. Its ornate interior design, which is inspired by the Kungliga Operan, adds to that elegant and royal feel of the club. When you get a little tired on the dance floor, you can also take a moment to relax at their beautiful open-air veranda. Have a couple drinks, sit back, and enjoy the view of Stockholm.

Södra Bar Website
https://www.facebook.com/SodraTeatern/
Södra Bar Map
https://goo.gl/maps/NQAiY436w742

Stampen
Location: Stora Nygatan 5, 111 27 Stockholm, Sweden
Opening Hours: 5:00 P.M. to 1:00 A.M. Tuesday – Friday
2:00 P.M. to 1:00 A.M. Saturday

If techno beats are not your thing and you just want some live jazz music to get your body dancing, then Stampen is the place for you. Its live jazz music with its good food, good beer, and good wine will definitely give you a great time.

Stampen Website
https://www.facebook.com/stampen.se/
Stampen Map
https://goo.gl/maps/X6JNsBzjR2x

13

Special Must-Try Activities

ABBA: The Museum & Swedish Music Hall of Fame
Location: Strömparrterren 3, 111 30 Stockholm, Sweden
Opening Hours: Varies widely, see website for details.
Phone:+46 8 121 328 60

Abba was a Swedish pop group that was responsible for international hits like Dancing Queen, Mamma Mia, Take a Chance on Me, and The Winner Takes It All, all of which are now a part of the popular musical Mamma Mia's soundtrack. If you want to discover the roots and the progression of Abba to global stardom, then you should pay ABBA: The Museum & Swedish Music Hall of Fame a visit while in Stockholm.

The Museum & Swedish Music Hall of Fame
http://www.abbathemuseum.com/en/groups-and-events-0
The Museum & Swedish Music Hall of Fame
https://goo.gl/maps/akTz28iVmvu

Boat Sightseeing

You have two options if you want to go sightseeing by boat in Stockholm. One, you can go with Strömma, where you have the chance to cruise under bridges of Stockholm while enjoying the views of the city. The other option is by Red, where you get to tour under 17 bridges in an hour and 45 minutes. You will also be taken to where the Baltic Sean and Lake Mälaren connect. Both sightseeing options also offer bus tours.

Phone:+46 8 120 040 00
Boat Sightseeing Website
http://www.stromma.se/en/stockholm/
sightseeing/sightseeing–by–boat/
Boat Sightseeing Map
https://goo.gl/maps/qb2wTPhBRuL2

Rooftop Hiking

Yes, hiking on a rooftop is another activity that you can do in Stockholm. For only $70, you can tour around Stockholm from a different view—the roofs. You can take pictures of the city skyline, unobstructed by the bustling streets down low. And even though selfie sticks are not allowed on this tour, guides are nice enough to take your group pictures for you.

Phone:+46 8 22 30 05
Rooftop Hiking Website

https://www.takvandring.com/en/home
Rooftop Hiking Map
https://goo.gl/maps/YKtwf8LnUzz

SkyView

Location: Ericsson Globen, Globentorget 2, Stockholm, Sweden
Opening Hours: 9:30 A.M. to 6:00 P.M. Weekdays
9:30 A.M. to 4:00 P.M. Weekends

In SkyView, you will have the chance to reach the peak of the world's largest spherical building. At 425 feet above sea level, you will also have the best view of Sweden's beautiful city.

Phone:+46 77 181 10 00
SkyView Website
http://www.globearenas.se/skyview/om-skyview
SkyView Map
https://goo.gl/maps/CY4UzBXxSpR2

Winter Activities

Stockholm is also beautiful during the winter. There are a lot of activities that you can do including 1) getting a room in one of their 200 ski resorts, 2) tracking some wolves, reindeers and bears on a safari, 3) spending a night in an actual igloo, 4) driving a dog sled, 5) catching fish from a frozen lake, 6) riding a snowmobile on a frozen river, and lastly, 7) seeing the majestic Northern Lights in the sky.

Ski Stockholm Website
https://www.skistar.com/en/Hammarbybacken/
About-Hammarbybacken/
Ski Stockholm Map
https://goo.gl/maps/5VPB7iJQDcv
Phone:+46 8 641 68 30

Safari Website
http://www.wildsweden.com/
Safari Map
https://goo.gl/maps/pq5ΛXbdoGjH2
Phone:+46 70 610 61 50

Igloo Website (ice hotel)
http://www.icehotel.com/about-icehotel/
Ice Bar Website
http://www.icebarstockholm.se/en/
Ice Bar Map
https://goo.gl/maps/dFQ4JYPKFjy
Phone:+46 8 505 635 20

Dog Sledding Website
http://dogsleddinginsweden.com/
Phone:+46 644 700 06

Fishing Sweden Website
http://www.fishing-in-sweden.com/

Sweden Adventures Website
https://www.whitetrailadventures.com/

Phone:+46 (0)730 469 304

Northern Lights Sweden Website
https://www.theaurorazone.com/destinations/
northern-lights-holidays-to-sweden
Phone:01670 785012

14

Travel Safety Tips

Have you booked a trip to Stockholm yet? Before you leave for a vacation to this foreign city, make sure to follow these travel safety tips in order to keep you and your belongings safe during your holiday.

Make copies of your passport and bring a couple with you when you travel. If your real passport gets lost or is stolen, you still need something to prove your citizenship. Also, leave a copy of your passport back home, either in your residence or with a trusted friend. It will also help if you have a digital copy of your passport in your mobile device and/or email.

See your doctor and ask if you need to get shots before you leave. For the trip, you should also ask for a prescription of your regular medications, if you are taking any.

Check-in with your medical insurance to see if it applies for international travel. If not, it is advisable to get additional insurance for your trip.

Find out what the exchange rate is beforehand. As of writing this book, a Swedish Krona is equal to 12 cents in the US Dollar. It is important that you have an idea of what the exchange rate is so you won't be ripped off when you convert your money. Also, a bank or an ATM will be your best option for exchanging currency. Most conversion centers apply additional fees.

Exchange Rate Website
http://www.xe.com/currencyconverter/

Call your bank before you leave and inform them that you are traveling. In the middle of your vacation, your credit card provider might turn off your card without warning, thinking that your transactions are fraud. It is also wise to call your provider to ask if your credit card will work overseas.

Lastly, inform a friend or family member about your trip. Leave them with your departure and arrival details, as well as your itinerary for your entire trip. In the case of an emergency, they will know which hotel to call and where you are supposed to be going while you are away.

15

Three-Day Itinerary

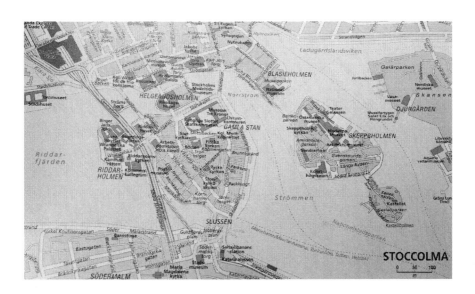

Day 1: History and Culture

Check-in at your hotel and immediately tour around the city. Start with a boat sightseeing tour of Stockholm's historical landmarks such as the City Hall, the Royal Palace, and Gamla Stan.

After the boat sightseeing tour, you can travel by bus or train to Medeltidsmuseet or the Vasa Museet to get a better sense of Stockholm's colorful history. In the evening, you can then unwind by buying a couple drinks at one of Stockholm's bars that were listed on this book.

Day 2: Food and Arts

You can spend day 2 by going on a culinary trip around the city. Take a tour around the city's cafés and taste their delicious cups of fika. Eat at some of the restaurants listed on this travel guide as well. You can also find street vendors selling food in carts.

While on this culinary adventure, why don't you also take a trip around the museums and art galleries listed on this book? Be amazed by the beauty in pictures at Fotografiska, appreciate contemporary and modern art over at Medeltidsmuseet, and get astonished by the innovative and inventive lives of the Nobel Laureates over at the Nobel Museet.

If you're still energized to do something in the nighttime, go dancing at one of the nightclubs listed on this book. There's no better way to end the evening than with a couple of delicious drinks, some good music, and a crowded dance floor to keep you company.

Day 3: Other Activities

Day 3 is the day to just enjoy the city and soak in its beauty. Visit a park and appreciate the greenery of the city, or have some fun by doing any of the activities listed on Chapter 12. Before you leave Stockholm, make sure to take a lot of pictures of its beautiful architecture and historical landscape so you have something to remember your trip by.

16

Conclusion

Now that you have reached the end of this travel guide, you should have a clearer idea of what a weekend in Stockholm has in store for you.

There are still a lot of sights, galleries, and restaurants that did not make it on the top 5 lists, and that only proves how worthwhile your travel to this beautiful city will be.

Lastly, if you like this book, please rate it on Amazon.

Thank you once again for downloading this book! I hope that through this travel guide, you have learned enough about Stockholm, Sweden to convince you to pay this wonderful city a visit the next time you are in Europe.

Made in the USA
Columbia, SC
17 October 2021